THE GREAT SPHINX OF GIZA
THE PHARAOHS' ETERNAL GUARDIAN

History Kids Books
Children's Ancient History

BABY PROFESSOR
EDUCATION KIDS

Speedy Publishing LLC

40 E. Main St. #1156

Newark, DE 19711

www.speedypublishing.com

Copyright 2017

In this book, we're going to talk about the Great Sphinx of Giza. So, let's get right to it!

WHAT IS THE GREAT SPHINX OF GIZA?

In Egypt, in the city of Giza, not far from the city of Cairo, there is a monumental statue that sits south of the Pharaoh Khafre's Pyramid. It has the head of a Pharaoh and the body of a lion with massive front paws. It's called the Great Sphinx of Giza.

The Great Sphinx of Giza

SERVANT STATUE

This ancient sculpture has become a symbol of Egypt, both past and present. It appears on Egyptian coins, stamps, and formal documents. It has inspired adventurers and archaeologists over the centuries.

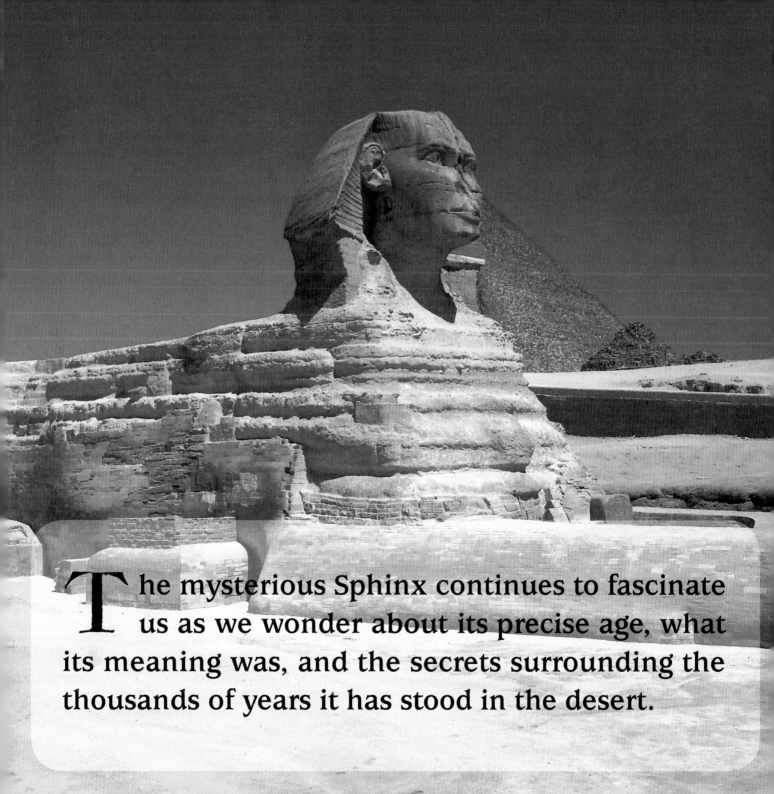

The mysterious Sphinx continues to fascinate us as we wonder about its precise age, what its meaning was, and the secrets surrounding the thousands of years it has stood in the desert.

WHAT DOES THE WORD SPHINX MEAN?

The ancient Greeks had a sphinx in their mythology as well. The Greek sphinx had a woman's head, a lion's body, and a bird's wings. She posed riddles and would kill those who couldn't provide the answer.

The word "sphinx" means "strangler" or "to hold fast" so perhaps the sphinx had her victims in a stranglehold because they couldn't solve her riddles. The origins of the word could also have come from the fact that lionesses strangle their prey to death.

Thousands of sphinx sculptures were built in Egypt. They generally have the same type of figure with the head of a man and body of a lion. There are some that have the heads of rams, and these types of sphinxes were created to give reverence to the god Amun, the main god of all the Egyptian gods.

We don't know the name that the Sphinx had during ancient times.

WHEN WAS IT BUILT?

There was a stone quarry at the location on the plateau where the Sphinx now sits. It's believed that the Pharaoh's workers sculpted the limestone there to create the massive monument.

Although archaeologists have disagreed about the time frame, most believe it was sculpted around 2500 BC, during the reign of the Pharaoh Khafre in the period of Egypt's civilization called the Old Kingdom. It's also believed the face carved on the lion's body was the face of the Pharaoh Khafre.

Pharaoh Khafre

DREAM STELE

There is a stele called a Dream Stele that sits right between the Sphinx's paws. A stele is a stone tablet that is something like a tombstone. Some Egyptologists believe Khafre's father, the Pharaoh Khufu, who was the builder of Giza's Great Pyramid, could have also been responsible for having the Sphinx built.

The Sphinx's head and its face definitely show an artistic style that belonged to the Old Kingdom period in Egypt's history, especially the 4th Dynasty. The face is square-shaped and broad and has a broad chin as well.

The type of headdress depicted on the Sphinx was called a "nemes" that was a striped garment. It had a fold positioned at the top of the Pharaoh's head with triangularly shaped planes positioned in back of the ears that hung down upon the shoulders. There is also a "uraeus," which is the sacred symbol of the cobra.

WHY WAS IT BUILT?

In general, the Egyptians built sphinxes as guardians to their important buildings, either tombs or temples. There's evidence that one of the reasons the Giza's Sphinx was built was to associate the Pharaoh Khafre with the main god of the sun. It faces the rising sun and guards the pyramids of Giza.

Just compare the size of the people and the sphinx

HOW BIG IS THE SPHINX AND IS THERE ANYTHING INSIDE IT?

The Sphinx is enormous in size. It's 241 feet in length and 66 feet tall. The eyes on the face are as tall as a 6-foot man and the ears are more than three feet in height. The nose would have been about five feet in length.

It was sculpted directly from the bedrock, and the colors of the stone range from a soft yellow hue to a hard gray color. The body was made from the softer stone and the head was made of the harder gray stone. The head has remained in overall better condition than the huge seated body, which has suffered a lot of erosion over time.

The lower body was made of enormous blocks of stone from the quarry. The ancient engineers used those same types of blocks for building the temples nearby as well. They excavated around the original outcrop of rock and removed these huge blocks that weighed tons.

It's still not known precisely how the ancient builders were able to move these enormous stones. Because of the method that was used to construct the Sphinx, modern carbon dating to determine its age can't be guaranteed to be accurate.

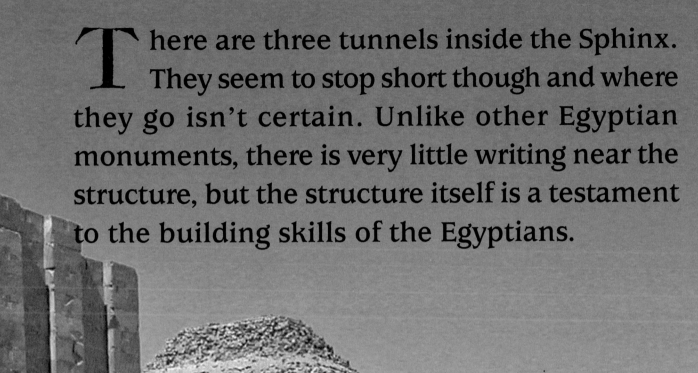

There are three tunnels inside the Sphinx. They seem to stop short though and where they go isn't certain. Unlike other Egyptian monuments, there is very little writing near the structure, but the structure itself is a testament to the building skills of the Egyptians.

There has been a lot of speculation that there are chambers inside the Sphinx or caves or buildings underground. As more restoration work takes place, it's possible that more secrets about the Sphinx will be uncovered.

WHAT HAPPENED TO THE SPHINX'S NOSE?

No one is exactly sure how the Sphinx lost its nose. Some people believe that the nose was destroyed by someone or a group of people who believed the Sphinx was evil. Other stories say that soldiers from Turkey shot the nose off the monument.

There was even a theory that Napoleon's soldiers had been responsible, but pictures have been found that prove that the nose was already gone long before Napoleon's arrival in Egypt. Perhaps we will never know exactly what happened.

HOW DID IT LOOK WHEN IT WAS FIRST COMPLETED?

In addition to having a detailed face with all its facial features, the Sphinx more than likely was painted when it was first created or when it was later restored. It also would have had a beard that was long and braided.

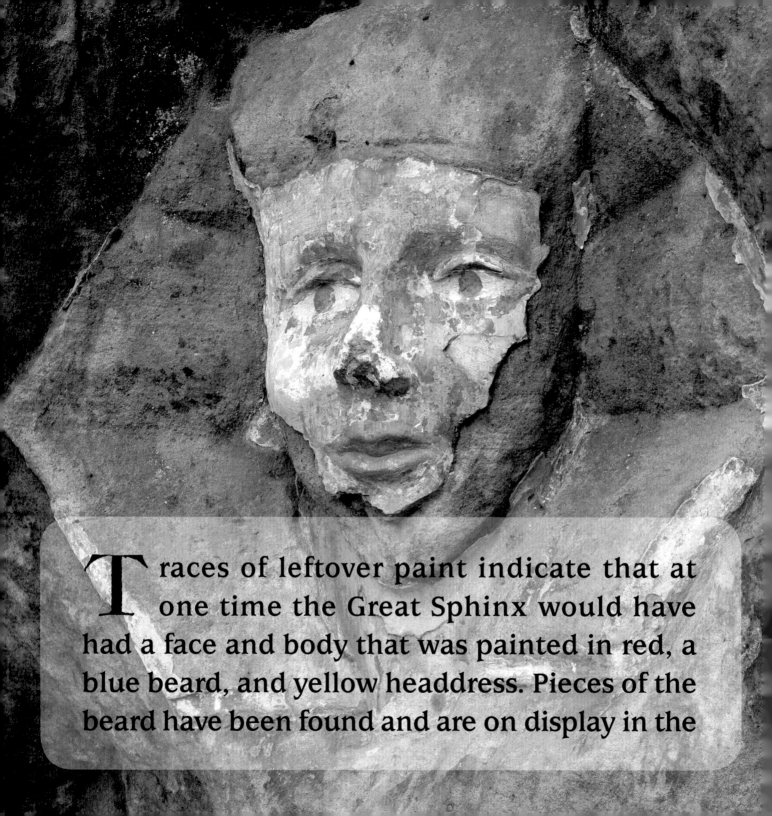

Traces of leftover paint indicate that at one time the Great Sphinx would have had a face and body that was painted in red, a blue beard, and yellow headdress. Pieces of the beard have been found and are on display in the

British Museum located in London as well as the Cairo Museum in Egypt. The beard was possibly added many years after the original Sphinx was created.

Dream Stele

THE LEGEND OF THE SPHINX

Over time the Egyptians worshipped the Great Sphinx as the representation of a god or gods called Horemakhet-Khepri-Ra-Atum. The translation of "Horemakhet" is "Horus, the sky god on the horizon."

Khepri meant the rising sun god and Ra-Atum was the god of the morning, midday, and evening sun. The Sphinx represented wisdom as well as the powerful sun gods. At the base of the lion's paws is a Dream Stele that tells an amazing story in hieroglyphics.

KHEPRI

GREAT SPHINX SLIGHTLY
COVERED WITH SAND DUNES

About 1,000 years after the Great Sphinx was built, it was covered in sand dunes and hadn't been properly maintained. A young prince by the name of Thutmose was hunting and he paused near the Sphinx and fell asleep in the shadow of its head.

When the sun was at its height in the sky, the noble god spoke to him. He told Thutmose that he was his father and that he was in poor condition. He asked Thutmose to restore him to his former glory and that if Thutmose took care of this that he would be rewarded and would become Pharaoh of the land. Thutmose restored the Sphinx to its earlier grandeur and became Pharaoh Thutmose IV around 1401 BC.

RA GOD OF THE SUN

FASCINATING FACTS ABOUT THE GREAT GIZA SPHINX

- The Sphinx has a long tail that wraps around one of its hind paws.

- In modern times, it was 1905 when removal of the sand was started so that the body of the Sphinx could be seen again.

- The Great Sphinx is thought to be the oldest monument ever built.

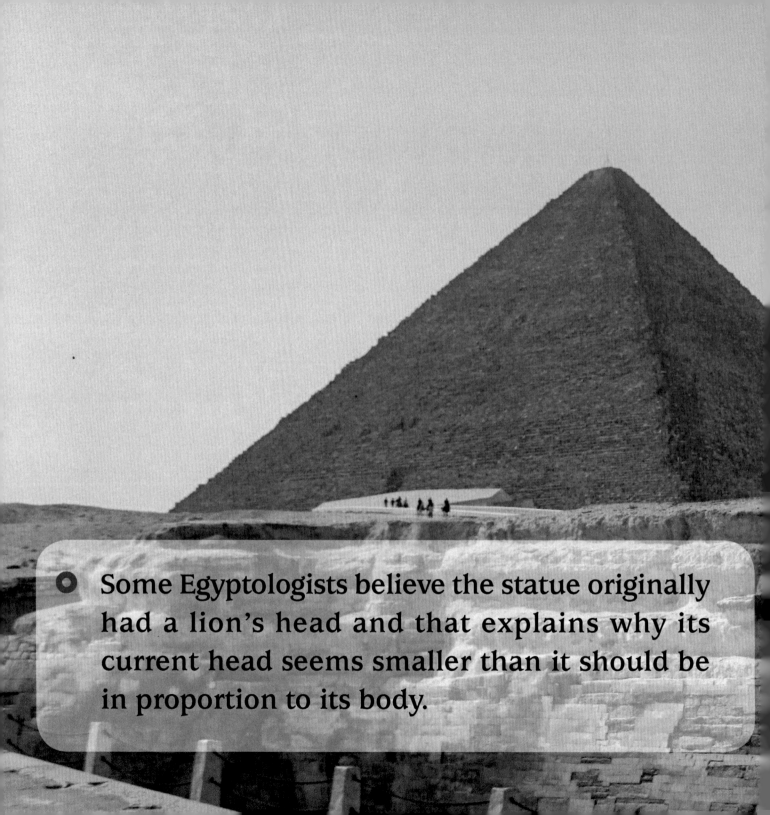

Some Egyptologists believe the statue originally had a lion's head and that explains why its current head seems smaller than it should be in proportion to its body.

There was a hole in the Sphinx's head that has now been filled. It's thought that this could have been for other decorations.

- The Sphinx has a lot of water damage. It's not clear how this water damage occurred and it's still being debated. From 10,000 to 5,000 BC there was a huge amount of rainfall in the area that is now the Sahara Desert, but this would mean that the Sphinx is much older than most people believe.

Awesome! Now you know more about one of Egypt's amazing monuments, the Great Giza Sphinx. You can find more Ancient History books from Baby Professor by searching the website of your favorite book retailer.

Visit

BABY PROFESSOR
EDUCATION KIDS

www.BabyProfessorBooks.com

to download Free Baby Professor eBooks
and view our catalog of new and exciting
Children's Books